Discover Jesus

in
Genesis

Larry Edison

Illustrated by
Deborah Obeid

WINEPRESS WP PUBLISHING

Dedication

For my wife, Jeanne,
who has given me the freedom to devote myself to a variety of projects, and has loved,
supported, and encouraged me through thick and thin.
Larry Edison

To my parents, Lee and Leonore Dowlen:
Thank you for your unconditional love and never-ending encouragement.
Deborah Obeid

My gratitude to the Scutts, who gave me the idea for this book and my sincere thanks to the
many who took time to read through the manuscript and offer their suggestions (Dave Sturkey,
Dave, Lisa, Jake and Jonah Heerdt, Julia Graham, Richard & RoseMarie Schminke, David &
Joanne Miller and Jerry Meyer) and to Daryl Davis who gave us the idea
for a number of these illustrations.

We are grateful for the opportunity the people of Covenant Life have given us
in receiving and encouraging our ministry and work we do in their midst.

© 2002 by Larry Edison, Illustrated by Deborah Obeid. All rights reserved.

Printed in Sarasota, FL by Palm Printing.

Packaged by WinePress Publishing, PO Box 428, Enumclaw, WA 98022. The views expressed or
implied in this work do not necessarily reflect those of WinePress Publishing. The author and
illustrator are ultimately responsible for the design, content, and editorial accuracy of this work.

Unless otherwise noted all Scriptures are taken from the Holy Bible, New International Version,
Copyright © 1973, 1978, 1984 by the International Bible Society. Used by permission of
Zondervan Publishing House. The "NIV" and "New International Version" trademarks are
registered in the United States Patent and Trademark Office by International Bible Society.

ISBN 1-57921-389-8
Library of Congress Catalog Card Number: 2001090402

Discover Jesus in Genesis

"The New is in the Old contained, the Old is in the New explained."
—*Augustine of Hippo*

This small work is designed to help you understand the Book of Genesis as it unveils and foreshadows Jesus, the promised Messiah. It is also intended as a means by which you can easily teach your children these same truths. There is a tendency for Christians to see Jesus only in the pages of the New Testament. The Old Testament, a vital part of the Bible, appears to some as an incomprehensible book—a jigsaw puzzle of unrelated stories. Many may fail to see the clear connection to the New Testament. Yet, as Jesus explained to His disciples on the road to Emmaus, all of the Scriptures speak of Him.

And beginning with Moses and all the Prophets, he explained to them what was said in all the Scriptures concerning himself. (Luke 24:27)

All the Old Testament is a foreshadow or promise of the coming of the Messiah. All that God did with His people Israel was designed to teach them of His grace, and what they were to expect with the coming of the Messiah. Through real-life events the people of Israel were given pictures concerning Jesus and his future work.

The people of Israel should have been prepared for the coming of Jesus. Yet, when Jesus came into the world, "His own did not receive Him." Though the way was paved by God's grace throughout history, most people ultimately wanted nothing to do with Jesus.

The Seed and the Tree

The Old Testament is like a seed that, with the coming of the New Testament, has grown into a fully blossoming tree. As this "seed" slowly takes root and grows into a tree, the wonders of Jesus are slowly, but surely, revealed. In the New Testament—the full-grown tree—we see the magnificent wonders of the Messiah in all His fullness. This seed growing into a full blossoming plant is what this book is all about. In academic studies, this is called "Biblical Theology."

The Garden and the City

Another way to illustrate the comparison between the Old and New Testaments is the progress of growth from a garden to a city. Genesis begins with a garden, and the Book of Revelation ends with a city, the New Jerusalem. This development from garden to city is to teach the idea of progress and the growth of the kingdom of God and the revelation of Jesus as Lord.

As you read this book, you will see how God carefully instructed His people about the Messiah's coming. You will find this especially evident while looking at the Old Testament with the glasses of the New. This provides the classic "twenty-twenty" perspective which hindsight gives.

All Scripture is rich with treasures of grace. God has given us these wonderful stories for our sake.

Larry Edison

Creation: The Beginning

In the beginning God created the heavens and the earth. (Genesis 1:1)
In the beginning was the Word, and the Word was with God, and the Word
was God. (John 1:1)

God created the heavens and the earth by His word. He spoke and said, "Let there be trees," and sure enough, there were trees. He said, "Let there be animals," and animals appeared on the earth.

God's word was the means by which creation sprang to life. Out of nothing God called creation into existence—a wonderful example of His power and creativity.

When we examine the Scriptures, we find that Christ participated in creation. Looking back at creation through the viewpoint of the New Testament, we can clearly see that it was Jesus who spoke the words of creation. Everything sprang into existence by Christ's word.

John's Gospel begins by identifying Jesus as God's Word. Calling Jesus "God's Word" is like saying that Jesus is God's voice. He was that voice calling into the darkness and creating the lights in the sky, the land, and the animals. Jesus, according to the Apostle John, was God's Word spoken at creation, but now come in flesh and blood (John 1:14).

Think ahead to the New Testament for just a moment. Mark records an event that demonstrates the power of Jesus' spoken word.

He got up, rebuked the wind and said to the waves, "Quiet! Be still!"
Then the wind died down and it was completely calm. (Mark 4:39)

Simply by the power of His word, Jesus could command the wind and the waves to calm down. The word spoken by God as seen in Genesis 1 is the same word spoken by Jesus who still remains in control of all creation. Because Jesus is God, Jesus can also be referred to as God's voice or as the mouthpiece of God.

According to the Bible, not only was Jesus present at creation, but also He was active and working. Through the New Testament Scriptures we see that it was Jesus who created all things.

For by him all things were created: things in heaven and on earth,
visible and invisible, whether thrones or powers or rulers or authorities;
all things were created by him and for him. (Colossians 1:16)

Jesus was there at creation as the author of life.

You killed the author of life, but God raised him from the dead. We are
witnesses of this. (Acts 3:15)

The Author of Life and the One raised from the dead can only be Jesus. No one can be the author of life apart from the One who called creation into existence.

When everything was formed Jesus was there. He was there with the Father creating all that exists, and so we owe Him our lives and our gratitude.

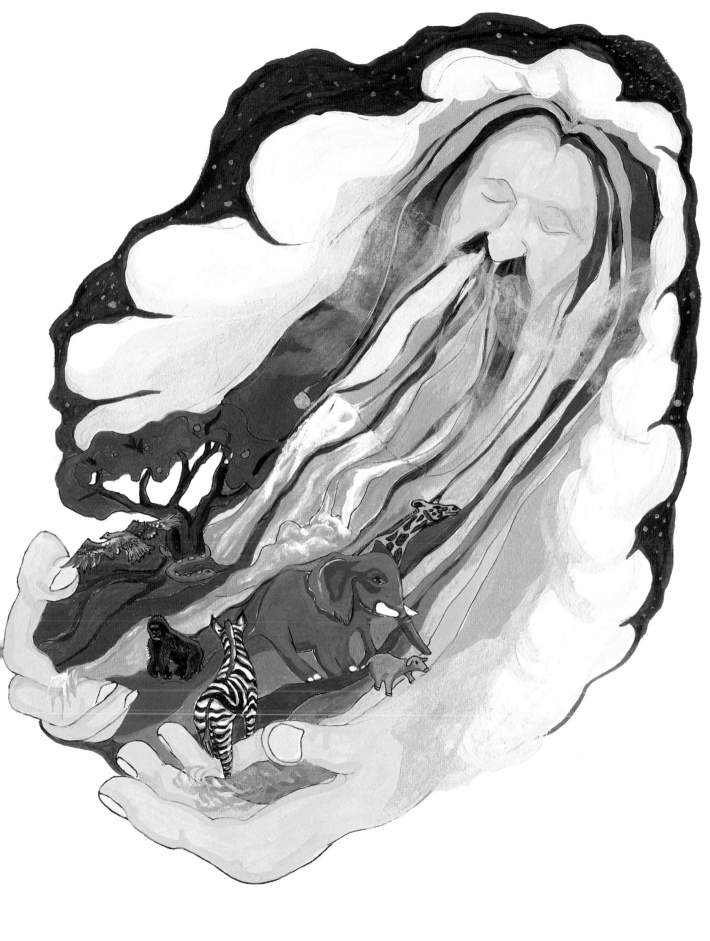

Crowned with Glory

> God blessed them and said to them, "Be fruitful and increase in number; fill the earth and subdue it. Rule over the fish of the sea and the birds of the air and over every living creature that moves on the ground." (Genesis 1:28)
>
> On his robe and on his thigh he has this name written: KING OF KINGS AND LORD OF LORDS. (Revelation 19:16)

God created Adam to be the ruler of His creation. As the "lord" of this creation he was told, along with his wife Eve, to subdue and tame creation for God's glory and his own enjoyment. God told him to:

> . . . fill the earth and subdue it. Rule over the fish of the sea and the birds of the air and over every living creature that moves on the ground. (Genesis 1:28)

Adam and Eve were created to rule. God told them to be fruitful, multiply, and fill the earth. Under the King of Kings, who was Christ Himself, they were king and queen of creation.

The entire earth would be their domain. Caring for God's creation was their responsibility. They were to cause it to flourish, and bring forth all its potential. By populating the earth they would bring the entire earth under humanity's domain. Adam and Eve were told to name the animals as God caused them to parade before them. This act emphasized that God placed Adam and Eve above all else in the world. They stood in wonder of His great work of creation.

Psalm 8:3–8 gives us a birds-eye view of creation from this perspective:

> When I consider your heavens, the work of your fingers . . . what is man that you are mindful of him, the son of man that you care for him? You made him a little lower than the heavenly beings and crowned him with glory and honor. You made him ruler over the works of your hands; you put everything under his feet: all flocks and herds . . . the birds of the air, and the fish of the sea, . . .

The writer of Hebrews quotes from this passage (Hebrews 2:6) and applies these words to Jesus. Why would this text from the Old Testament, originally speaking of Adam, be applied to Jesus? Hebrews tells us that this passage is not simply speaking of humanity, but especially of the person of Jesus. It is as though all creation was made for Jesus (Colossians 1:16). It is Jesus who has been crowned with glory and honor. It is Jesus who has everything under His feet.

Adam, as he ruled over creation, was a foretaste of the time when Jesus, after His resurrection, would be crowned as King of kings and Lord of lords. Adam at creation is a picture of the One coming who would be greater than Adam. Adam ruled over all the earth. Jesus rules over all creation as earth's greatest King and Redeemer.

We will, when Christ returns, rule with Christ. We who belong to Christ by faith will rule over a perfect creation, just as God intended.

> You have made them to be a kingdom and priests to serve our God, and they will reign on the earth. (Revelation 5:10)

The Promised Battle

And I will put enmity between you and the woman, and between your offspring and hers; he will crush your head, and you will strike his heel. (Genesis 3: 15)

Even though God created everything good, there came a time when Adam and Eve decided to disobey God. God clearly told Adam and Eve that they were not to eat from one particular tree in the garden. They could eat anything else they saw, but not the fruit from the Tree of the Knowledge of Good and Evil. God made this very clear, and even told them they would die if they ate the fruit from that tree.

But, you know how it is with us—when someone in authority says "No!" at times we can be all the more eager to do it anyway. The Bible says that Eve was tricked, but Adam deliberately disobeyed. They both decided it was more important to do what they felt like doing rather than obey God. So, they both ate the fruit. After they ate, God came into the garden and called to them. They heard His voice, and knowing what they had done, ran and hid. Can you imagine anything more foolish than thinking they could hide from God by ducking behind some bushes? We can clearly see that rebellion against God leads to foolishness.

God must be true to His Word to do what He promised. Though they would be able to live a long time, Adam and Eve would grow weaker and weaker and eventually die. It would be the same with all the generations to follow. But, as God told them about the horrible things which would happen to creation because of their rebellion, God also promised something special. He promised that Jesus would come. Actually, God did not mention the name Jesus, but He did tell Adam and Eve that someone would come who would fix everything they had ruined. God promised that One would come who, though He would be hurt, would destroy all wickedness (Genesis 3:15).

Here's the way the promise would be fulfilled. There would be conflict between the people of God and the world down through the ages. But, eventually, God would send His Son. At the height of the conflict, His Son would be wounded while crushing the skull of the serpent. That wound was His death by crucifixion. But, death could not hold Jesus forever. Jesus was raised from the grave. His resurrection and ascension as Lord of all creation would be a deathblow to Satan and his power.

Revelation 12:9–11 describes how Jesus defeated Satan:

> The great dragon was hurled down—that ancient serpent called the devil or Satan, who leads the whole world astray. He was hurled to the earth, and his angels with him. Then I heard a loud voice in heaven say: "Now have come the salvation and the power and the kingdom of our God, and the authority of his Christ. For the accuser of our brothers, who accuses them before our God day and night, has been hurled down. They overcame him by the blood of the Lamb and by the word of their testimony; . . .

Out of the Garden: Banished

So the Lord God banished him from the Garden of Eden . . . After he drove the man out, he placed on the east side of the Garden of Eden cherubim and a flaming sword flashing back and forth to guard the way to the tree of life. (Genesis 3:23–24)
And so Jesus also suffered outside the city gate to make the people holy through his own blood. (Hebrews 13:12)

Both Adam and Eve decided to live as though they were gods. They ate of the fruit as if they were accountable to no one. But in so doing, it was as though they raised their fists in God's face, and ate as a challenge to His power.

Though God continued to love them, they had to be disciplined. God couldn't warn them about punishment and then pretend as if nothing happened. God forced Adam and Eve from the garden. They were people in exile. He even placed an angel at the entrance of the garden to make sure they could not get back in. If they tried, they would die. No one would ever be allowed to enter God's presence again unless God provided a way to return.

In the same manner, generations later, the people of Israel were told that if they turned their backs on the Lord, they would be scattered from their land, and would enter a time of exile.

The Lord will scatter you among the peoples, and only a few of you will survive among the nations to which the Lord will drive you. (Deuteronomy 4:27) Then the Lord will scatter you among all nations, from one end of the earth to the other. There you will worship other gods—gods of wood and stone, which neither you nor your fathers have known. (Deuteronomy 28:64)

God would not allow Israel in His presence if they persisted in rebellion and sin. They were eventually driven from His presence and from their land into exile.

Now, think ahead to the account of Jesus' death. The political and religious leaders forced Him to walk outside the city of Jerusalem to be hung on a cross to die. When people during Jesus' day were punished for terrible crimes, their punishment always happened outside the city. This was the way of doing to criminals, what God did to Adam and Eve. When someone was taken out of Jerusalem to die, it was just as if they were leaving the presence of God and the company of God's people. It meant they were all alone, separated from God. When Jesus took His cross and walked outside of the city to die, it was just as if He were the One forced from the garden. He was being forced out of God's presence to suffer in the place of disobedient people—disobedient people like us.

The city called the New Jerusalem pictured at the end of the Bible is only for those who live in God's presence—those who have returned to God's presence His way. Those who belong to Jesus will be with Him forever. Those outside God's city are the people who did not trust Him or acknowledge Him as Lord in this life.

The following verse tells us who are the people outside God's city.

Blessed are those who wash their robes, that they may have the right to the tree of life and may go through the gates into the city. Outside are the dogs, those who practice magic arts, the sexually immoral, the murderers, the idolaters and everyone who loves and practices falsehood. (Revelation 22:14–15)

Murder near Paradise

> Now Cain said to his brother Abel, "Let's go out to the field." And while they were in the field, Cain attacked his brother Abel and killed him. (Genesis 4:8) But this is to fulfill what is written in their Law: "They hated me without reason." (John 15:25)

It did not take long for sin to grow and spread. Among the many children of Adam and Eve, Cain and Abel were two. You might imagine they were brothers who would normally love each other.

Yet Cain became jealous of Abel. In a world in which people were left to their own ways, Cain's jealousy fought for control. Even though God warned him, in a jealous rage he murdered his own brother. A sinful world is a world where brother will turn against brother, and children will turn against their parents.

The Apostle John wrote about the coming of Jesus that "He came to his own, but his own did not receive him." Not only did His own people reject Jesus, but also His own people cried out for His death. He was killed by His own, with the help of the Romans, just as Abel was murdered by his own brother. Cain had no other way to get at God, so he took his anger out on Abel. That is what the world has been doing with God's people for all of history. It is also the reason Christ died. Christ's death was the death of THE Innocent One at the hands of people who were angry with God and wanted to live in darkness rather than the light.

When Abel was killed, Adam and Eve's hope must have been dashed. They probably assumed that the promised Messiah would be one of their children, perhaps Cain or Abel. But, now Abel was dead and Cain was a murderer. In the death of Jesus it was as if history repeated itself. When Jesus died, everyone was confused as they hoped He was the Messiah. With His death hopes were shattered and dreams were crushed.

After His resurrection, His disciples came to understand that His death was not the last word—Jesus was the Messiah. Jesus was raised from the grave, proving He was the Messiah. On the day of Pentecost, Peter said, about the resurrection:

> Therefore let all Israel be assured of this: God has made this Jesus, whom you crucified, both Lord and Christ. (Acts 2:36)

Throughout the Bible we are shown that whenever the world persecutes the Church, the world is ultimately persecuting Jesus and trying to get rid of Him. The murder of Abel by Cain is typical of the manner in which the world would respond to Jesus. Look at the words of the Psalmist as he laments this same problem and pleads with God for help.

> See how your enemies are astir, how your foes rear their heads. With cunning they conspire against your people; they plot against those you cherish. . . . With one mind they plot together; they form an alliance against you— (Psalm 83:2-5)

The Flood

Now the earth was corrupt in God's sight and was full of violence. . . . So God said to Noah, "I am going to put an end to all people, for the earth is filled with violence because of them. I am surely going to destroy both them and the earth. (Genesis 6:11,13)
For in the days before the flood, people were eating and drinking, marrying and giving in marriage, up to the day Noah entered the ark; and they knew nothing about what would happen until the flood came and took them all away. That is how it will be at the coming of the Son of Man. (Matthew 24:38-39)

Everyone was surprised when the flood came—that is, everyone but Noah. Most of the people living on the earth had become so wicked and violent that God could not stand it anymore. Noah and his family, the only believers left who loved the Lord, were all surrounded by wickedness. God wanted to protect Noah by getting rid of the wickedness and its influence. He would not allow Noah's family to be overwhelmed with people who were a terrible influence and who might eventually lead even them astray.

God promised to send a flood that would cover the earth with water. It took Noah and his family 120 years to build a boat big enough keep them and many animals safe. For those 120 years Noah warned the rest of the people about what was coming, but no one listened. They all laughed at Noah and continued in their immoral and destructive ways.

Then, after all those years of preparation, the rains started and the flood came. Except for Noah and his family, everyone else drowned. God protected the people He loved from the influence of the corrupt people. That's why the Apostle Peter writes:

. . . who disobeyed long ago when God waited patiently in the days of Noah while the ark was being built. In it only a few people, eight in all, were saved through water. (1 Peter 3:20)

We think that it was the ark—the boat—that saved Noah. But really, it was the flood, because the water swept away all those who were trying to get Noah and his family to disobey God along with them. The flood washed away the evil influence that threatened to destroy his family spiritually and morally.

The flood teaches us about Jesus. On the very last day of history Jesus will come back. Many, many people laugh and ridicule that idea. There are those who ignore God's commands and live as though there is no God. But, like the sudden judgment during the time of Noah, Jesus will come back suddenly. When He does return, the wicked and unbelieving people who do not believe Jesus will be punished forever. But those who know and trust the Savior will be protected from this punishment, just as Noah was protected. The flood came upon the earth so that people would know that someday Jesus himself would come back. The fact that there was a flood should cause us to pay attention to Jesus who has promised to come back again. His coming will take some by surprise, even as the flood was a surprise to those who were not listening to the Lord. We have been warned so we can prepare for that great meeting by trusting in Jesus.

The Promise of Protection: The Rainbow

I have set my rainbow in the clouds, and it will be the sign of the covenant between me and the earth. Whenever I bring clouds over the earth and the rainbow appears in the clouds, I will remember my covenant between me and you and all living creatures of every kind. Never again will the waters become a flood to destroy all life. (Genesis 9:13–15)

God promised never to destroy creation in that same manner after the flood. God would protect His people in other ways. Ever since the flood, God's promise has been displayed in the sky. When we see a rainbow, we are reminded of the promise God made that He would protect His people from complete destruction. Actually, it was a reminder for God. Scripture says that God will see the rainbow, and it will be reminder for Him. We see the rainbow and feel a sense of security, knowing God is reminded of His promise.

God promised that His people would be kept safe. The promise of safety was given so that Jesus could be born. In Genesis 3:15 we saw that God foretold the coming of Messiah. The world would go on for Jesus' sake. Ultimately, Jesus was the reason for the rainbow, as well as the foundation on which God's promise rests. God will protect His people until Christ's return.

The story of people began in the Garden of Eden, but will end with what the Bible describes as the New Jerusalem (Revelation 3:12; 22:14–19). The history of God's people has been a history of an earthly journey, which began in a garden and will be completed in the new city.

When God displays His rainbow in the sky, we are to remember that God protects His people. If not for Jesus, God would have to destroy the world because of sin. God's tolerance for sin would come to an end, were it not for His wrath being pacified by Jesus. Because God promised in Genesis that Jesus would come, He had to protect both the world and Christ's genealogical line so the promise of His coming could be fulfilled.

God promised that until the end of the world—until Jesus comes back for a second time—the earth will be spared from complete destruction. You have heard the song, "He's got the whole world in His hands." That's what the rainbow promises.

This is the plan determined for the whole world; this is the hand stretched out over all nations. For the LORD Almighty has purposed, and who can thwart him? His hand is stretched out, and who can turn it back? (Isaiah 14:26–27)

God has a perfect plan for this world—and a perfect plan for us. Nothing will keep God from doing all He has planned. The end result is that humanity will continue to live and flourish. Cultures will continue to develop, and people will continue to fill the earth (even as God intended in Genesis 1:26–28). Humanity will still suffer hardships and experience the curse in creation. But, we will be kept safe until He returns. That's the reason we have pictured the rainbow linking the garden and the city. We will, as a people, be kept safe from total destruction from the beginning to the very end of history.

The Tower of Confusion

. . . there the LORD confused the language of the whole world.
(Genesis 11:9) . . . we hear them declaring the wonders of God in our own
tongues! (Acts 2:11)

Long after the flood, when the earth was repopulated, arrogance and pride grew as fast as the new population. People began to think (just as Adam and Eve did) that they could be as powerful as God. In their arrogance a great number of people got together and found that when together they seemed stronger and more confident than when they were alone. "We're so powerful that nothing can stop anything we try," they thought. Determined to construct a building that would reach into the heavens, they thought they could rule the earth and be just like God.

That was vain and foolish—a sinful illusion. No person, or multitude of people, could be as strong and powerful as God. To show these people how absurd they were, God came down and confused their language. One minute they were working together and cooperating to build this tower. The next minute, when they opened their mouths to speak, they all began speaking strange and different languages. The building project came to an abrupt stop when they could not understand each other. Something as simple as a language barrier totally and completely put an end to their ineffectual dreams and plans.

Centuries later God came down again—He came in the flesh as the person of Jesus. After His death and resurrection, the Lord ascended into heaven. Forty days after His ascension He sent His Holy Spirit. On that Day of Pentecost the Spirit of Christ shook the disciples. These were the same disciples of Jesus who had assembled in worship, and when they opened their mouths to speak, they found that they were giving thanks to God in languages they had not previously learned. God instantly gave them the ability to speak in foreign languages, and understand each other. Unlike the events at the Tower of Babel, God was showing His followers (and us) that Jesus brings unity and not confusion in the midst of diversity.

 God brought people from many different countries to faith in Jesus that day—and made of them something new. At Babel, God was separating and driving people away from each other. But when we belong to Jesus, we are gathered and built together with people who are all different; yet part of His family—the Church.

Even though God confused people at Babel, Jesus would later bring people together. That's what the church is—people from varying backgrounds who are one because they belong to Jesus. Christ has broken down the barriers between people. The Church is to be the primary example of the way in which barriers between nations, races, and peoples can be broken and healed.

There is neither Jew nor Greek, slave nor free, male nor female, for you
are all one in Christ Jesus. (Galatians 3:28)

Those who try to build unity and stability apart from Christ are doomed to failure, even as those who tried, in vain, to build a tower that would reach to the heavens. God wants us to build a name for His glory, not ours.

God's Promise to Abraham

He took him outside and said, "Look up at the heavens and count the stars—
if indeed you can count them." Then he said to him, "So shall your offspring be." (Genesis 15:5)
A record of the genealogy of Jesus Christ the son of David, the son of
Abraham: (Matthew 1:1)
He redeemed us in order that the blessing given to Abraham might come to
the Gentiles through Christ Jesus, . . . The promises were spoken to Abraham
and to his seed. The Scripture does not say "and to seeds," meaning many
people, but "and to your seed," meaning one person, who is Christ.
(Galatians 3:14,16)

Abraham was a great-great-great grandson of Noah and an old man when God made him a promise. Abraham and Sarah were really too old to have children. Yet, God told them they were going to bear a nation of children. Here is how it happened. God told Abraham to look out at the sky. Abraham saw the stars lighting the eastern sky. While Abraham marveled at the stars, God promised him that he would have as many children as there were stars in the sky.

More than just children, God promised Abraham that these children would be a special nation, and would live in a land that God would give them. The land became known as the "Promised Land." The people living in the land would then (according to God's promise to Abraham in Genesis 12:1–3) be a blessing to all the other nations of the world.

But could this promise come true when Abraham was so old? Certainly! God can do all things. Abraham did have a child; his name was Isaac. When Isaac grew up, he had a boy named Jacob, and Jacob was the father of twelve sons. These sons were fathers of the twelve tribes of Israel. God counted as the children of Abraham all the people of the families of Israel. God was true to His word, and Abraham had an entire nation of children.

The promise does not stop there. From God's perspective, the child promised to Abraham was more than just his son Isaac. When God spoke to Abraham that late night and promised a son, though Abraham did not realize it, God was promising Abraham that Jesus would be born as Abraham's greatest son.

Jesus would be God's special blessing to all the world (Genesis 12:3). When people come to believe in Jesus, Abraham's greatest "Son," they are blessed and are given eternal life. If we believe in Jesus, then we also are counted as sons and daughters of Abraham.

Understand, then, that those who believe are children of Abraham. The
Scripture foresaw that God would justify the Gentiles by faith, and announced the gospel in advance to Abraham: "All nations will be blessed
through you." So those who have faith are blessed along with Abraham,
the man of faith. (Galatians 3:7–9)

God had us in mind when He promised Abraham that He would bless people from all nations! By means of the Gospel, the blessing of Abraham is spreading into the whole world.

Cut Off

Any uncircumcised male, who has not been circumcised in the flesh, will
be cut off from his people; he has broken my covenant. (Genesis 17:14)

When I think of cutting, I think of something that hurts. Although some cutting is destructive, some is actually helpful. Being cut by a sharp piece of glass can hurt and cause damage. Yet, a cut by a scalpel in the hands of a surgeon can bring relief and health. God uses the imagery of cutting throughout the Scriptures to help us understand something important about the way He treats His people.

Adam and Eve were exiled from the Garden and an angel with a flaming sword was placed at its entrance. If Adam and Eve had tried to return to the garden, they would have been cut through with the sword—which would have meant instant death.

The language of the Bible regarding covenant-making referred to cutting. Today we use the expression, "I'm going to make a covenant." But the language used in Bible times was: "I'm going to cut a covenant." Literally, God's covenant was to be cut onto Abraham's flesh and the flesh of his male descendants (Genesis 17:10–11). God added a sign to the covenant first announced in Genesis 12—a sign that Abraham and his family could clearly see. God's covenant promise, the promise of children, and the promise that these children would belong to God, would be cut into Abraham's flesh and his sons' flesh as a reminder throughout the generations. This happened first to Abraham as an adult, but his male children from then on were to be circumcised at eight days of age.

The cutting of the flesh in circumcision was a promise—a promise that God would be Abraham's God and the God of his descendants. But the cutting of the flesh was also God's warning that anyone who didn't believe in Him would be cut off from their people. People who disobeyed God's laws were people who didn't believe in Him, and that's why they were cut off.

Have you ever thought about what ultimate destruction would be like? God pictures ultimate judgment as being cut off from God's people and from the land of promise. This is also a picture of the judgment of hell. Hell is the experience of being completely cut off from the presence of the Lord, just as Adam and Eve were cut off from the garden.

When Abraham and Isaac were circumcised it was a promise of blessing, but also a promise of judgment if they were to abandon God's covenant. When Jesus died, He was cut off from His own people, the people of Israel, and killed outside the gates of Jerusalem. He was cut off from the presence of God the Father and cried out, "Why have you forsaken me?" At that moment, He suffered all the pains of hell. Jesus is the recipient of the ultimate circumcision in that He was cut off from life in our behalf. The covenant was cut in His blood, so that we would not have to die for our disobedience. As the knife cut Isaac's foreskin and drew blood, so the spear drew the blood of Jesus for us. Jesus is the great fulfillment of the covenant that was cut for us. He was cut off so we could be given life.

Abraham's Greatest Sacrifice

Then God said, "Take your son, your only son, Isaac, whom you love, and go to the region of Moriah. Sacrifice him there as a burnt offering on one of the mountains I will tell you about." (Genesis 22:2)
. . . he gave His one and only Son, . . . (John 3:16)

How sad Abraham must have been when he was told by God to sacrifice his beloved son. You would think his response would have been, "Anything but that Lord!" Can you imagine anything more horrible? How could God delight in human sacrifice?

Isaac was God's gift to Abraham and Sarah, and now God commanded Abraham to sacrifice that son. Even though in anguish, Abraham obeyed God and planned to carry out God's command. But just as Abraham's knife was poised to plunge down onto Isaac, God sent an angel to stop Abraham. God provided a substitute offering instead. The ram God provided and announced through the angel, and not Isaac himself, was to be offered as the sacrifice. By means of this offering, God was teaching Isaac—and us—about what it means that Jesus is our substitute.

John the Baptist saw Jesus coming toward him and called Him "the lamb of God." Isaac's ram was a foreshadow of Jesus' own sacrifice. Even as Isaac was Abraham's special son, so it was Jesus who was God's special Son. Both were called to die. Yet, because God provided Jesus as a lamb, Isaac did not have to die. Jesus was there with Abraham and Isaac. The lamb took Isaac's place just as Jesus took our place. There was no substitute for Jesus—He died as the Lamb of God.

God is no longer obliged to punish us for our sin, rebellion, and pride. Punishment has already been exacted. God provided a Lamb who bore the punishment that we deserve. It was Jesus, who was the One who was punished in our place. It was Jesus, who, like the ram in the briars, wore a crown of thorns for us. He was punished by the Father so we, who belong to Jesus by faith, would not have to be punished. That's how much He loves us. Just as the ram was stuck in the thorn bushes, so Jesus as the Lamb of God endured the thorns placed on His head. He suffered so we can live.

Also, just as Isaac seemingly received his life back again, so Jesus did as well. In Isaac's case, he escaped death. In Jesus' case, though He died, He was raised to new life. We can say that Jesus was there with Isaac because this entire event in Isaac's life was both a foreshadow of Jesus' death as a sacrifice on our behalf as well as a picture of His resurrection. Abraham knew God would raise Isaac to life, even if he had to carry out the sacrifice. He told his servant, "Stay here with the donkey while I and the boy go over there. We will worship and then we will come back to you" (Genesis 22:5). The writer of Hebrews affirms the same when he says, "Abraham reasoned that God could raise the dead, and figuratively speaking, he did receive Isaac back from death" (Hebrews 11:19).

Jacob's Stairway to Heaven

> He had a dream in which he saw a stairway resting on the earth, with its top reaching to heaven, and the angels of God were ascending and descending on it. (Genesis 28:12)
> . . . the angels of God ascending and descending . . . (John 1:51)

Jacob was in trouble. He was running from his older brother who wanted to harm him. Esau was enraged that Jacob had stolen his birthright, and even more so when he discovered that his own mother was part of the deception. Jacob was quite alone, in despair, and wondering what was going to happen to him. After traveling all day, he lay down to sleep and dreamt. In the dream he saw a ladder, or stairway, going all the way up into heaven. As he looked he saw angels moving up and down on the ladder. The angels were bringing him the promises of God. He felt quite safe, realizing he had God's promise to protect him and be with him. The ladder was not for Jacob to climb. The ladder, or stairway, was a picture of God taking the initiative to bless Jacob with all the blessings and protection of heaven.

God promised never to leave Jacob. This dream was God's way of giving panicky Jacob a sense of security. As Jacob was running away from home and certain death, God promised to always be with him and protect him. Through his father, Isaac, God promised to bless Jacob. In this dream, God was reaffirming this promise, even while Jacob was running scared and did not feel safe. God would make sure that the blessings of heaven made it to earth for Jacob.

> There above it stood the Lord, and he said: "I am the Lord, the God of your father Abraham and the God of Isaac. I will give you and your descendants the land on which you are lying. Your descendants will be like the dust of the earth, and you will spread out to the west and to the east, to the north and to the south. All peoples on earth will be blessed through you and your offspring. I am with you and will watch over you wherever you go, and I will bring you back to this land. I will not leave you until I have done what I have promised you." (Genesis 28:13–15)

Now, let's skip centuries into the future to a time when Jesus was beginning His public ministry. Jesus told a young man named Nathaniel that people would see angels traveling up and down on the Son of Man. Nathaniel caught the analogy with Jacob's ladder immediately. He understood that God was going to bring His people all the promises and blessings they would ever need—and they would all come through Jesus. The angels would bring God's grace and favor through Christ. Jesus would be the means by which the angels would be able to go to and from God's presence with grace.

Imagine the surprise experienced by Nathaniel! Jesus told Nathaniel that He Himself was Jacob's ladder. So long ago when Jacob was dreaming about the stairway, God was showing Jacob something about Jesus. It is through Jesus that God can let His love and care come to all His people. The ladder or stairway was really a picture of what Christ would do for Jacob. It would be through Jesus that Jacob, and we all along with Jacob, would be blessed and given God's promises.

Jesus was there with Jacob in the wilderness—He was Jacob's stairway. He is the reason God can give promises and provide good things for His people even now.

Rejected!

So when Joseph came to his brothers, they stripped him of his robe—the richly ornamented robe he was wearing— (Genesis 37:23)
". . . They hated me without reason." (John 15: 25)

If you had ten brothers and sisters, how would you feel if they ganged up on you and wanted to get rid of you? You'd no doubt feel rejected and alone. That must have been how Joseph felt when his brothers hurt him. They almost murdered him, but instead, threw him into a pit while deciding how to get rid of him. Though he was their brother, they sold him as slave, and strangers took him away from his home and family into Egypt.

Not only was Joseph sold as a slave, but also he was later imprisoned for something he did not do. He was a slave. He felt abandoned, and he was accused of a crime he did not commit. Yet, through all this, God was with Joseph. Eventually he was raised from certain death in prison and seated on the throne of power ruling and directing all the economic affairs of Egypt. Eventually Joseph was set free and promoted as one of the most powerful rulers in the land.

One reason why God allowed Joseph to experience these horrible and tragic events was to disclose what would happen to the Messiah. Jesus was going to be rejected by all those who were close to him. Even in the Garden, before His betrayal, with his closest friends, He was alone. He asked the disciples to stay awake while He prayed, but they fell asleep, abandoning Him to loneliness. When the soldiers came, all his friends deserted him and fled, leaving Him totally alone. Even while He was tortured and in pain, hanging from the cross, people hounded Him and took pleasure in His suffering.

Just as Joseph was alone, far from home for years while a captive in prison, so Jesus was alone and forsaken. Jesus also was accused of crimes He did not commit. It was the Father's plan that there would be no one on earth who would stand with Him and rescue Him from His suffering and death. Joseph was abandoned by his brothers, yet Jesus was abandoned and betrayed by everyone and left all alone.

At the end, He had no one on earth to whom He could turn. He was even abandoned by His Heavenly Father, and cried out, "My God, my God, why have you forsaken me?" This was predicted by the prophet Isaiah who said:

Yet it was the LORD's will to crush him and cause him to suffer, . . .
(Isaiah 53:10)

His words were an exact quote from Psalm 22 which reads:

"My God, my God, why have you forsaken me?"

The suffering of Christ was for us—for all who, by apathy or disobedience, have betrayed our Lord. He suffered the consequences of our rebellion and so was abandoned and betrayed. We, who belong to Christ, will never be abandoned by the Father, for Christ was abandoned in our place.

Just as this was not the final word for Joseph, it was not the final word for Christ. God had not finished what He planned.

Savior and Ruler of Egypt

They told him, "Joseph is still alive! In fact, he is ruler of all Egypt." Jacob was stunned; he did not believe them. (Genesis 45:26)
. . . and from Jesus Christ, who is the faithful witness, the firstborn from the dead, and the ruler of the kings of the earth. (Revelation 1:5)

After surviving the results of his brothers' hatred, Joseph found himself a prisoner. Accused of all kinds of wrongdoing, Joseph was thrown into jail by an Egyptian leader. From slavery to prison—not exactly what Joseph wanted. You might imagine that God had forgotten about poor Joseph. But God did not disregard his plight. All this was preparation for the moment when Joseph would be released from jail and promoted as a ruler over Egypt. When the king saw that God was with Joseph, that is exactly what happened. He was promoted to the second-highest position of authority in Egypt. Only the king himself had greater power. Joseph was in charge of everything that happened in the land of Egypt, and this was God's doing.

While Joseph was the ruler in Egypt, he met his brothers, who did not recognize him, as he was now an adult. After a time he revealed who he was, and instructed them to tell his father that he was still alive. At first they were terrified that Joseph would exact revenge on them. They went back to Canaan amazed, and told their father that they had seen Joseph. Certainly, Joseph's father and his brothers thought Joseph was dead. Yet, when the entire family gathered in his presence, they all bowed down in wonder and honored their brother, just as the dream said they would. Joseph became their savior because, with the power of God, he saved them, and all of Egypt with them, from starvation.

Joseph's life was a picture of what God was going to do with Jesus. Jesus was mistreated just like Joseph. But unlike Joseph, Jesus didn't simply spend time in a jail. He was actually killed. Both experienced a type of resurrection. Just as Joseph was raised from prison to become a powerful ruler, so Jesus was raised from death and the grave to become the most powerful person in all of the universe. This is also consistent with a theme found in the Bible of suffering before experiencing glory. After His suffering, He gained the title of "King of kings and Lord of lords." Joseph became a savior and a lord of his family and all Egypt, just as Jesus is the Savior and Lord of all who call upon Him. When people bowed before Joseph, without knowing it they were actually bowing to Jesus who placed Joseph on that throne.

This is a picture or a glimpse of the future time when all people from all nations of the earth will bow before Christ. They will recognize Him at His coming and will bow as He is seated on His throne in glory.

I saw heaven standing open and there before me was a white horse, whose rider is called Faithful and True. With justice he judges and makes war. His eyes are like blazing fire, and on his head are many crowns . . . his name is the Word of God. The armies of heaven were following him, riding on white horses and dressed in fine linen, white and clean. Out of his mouth comes a sharp sword with which to strike down the nations. "He will rule them with an iron scepter." . . . On his robe and on his thigh he has this name written: KING OF KINGS AND LORD OF LORDS. (Revelation 19:11–16)

Suggested Reading

If you are interested in further reading on this subject, I would recommend the following books:

1. Clowney, Edmund. *The Unfolding Mystery: Discovering Christ in the Old Testament.* NavPress, Colorado Springs, CO, 1988.

2. DeGraaf, S. G. *Promise and Deliverance.* Volumes 1–4, Presbyterian and Reformed Publishing Co., Phillipsburg, NJ, 1978.

3. Mahan, Henry. *With New Testament Eyes: Pictures of Christ in the Old Testament.* Evangelical Press, Durham, England, 1993.

4. Radius, Marianne. *The Tent of God—A Journey Through the Old Testament.* Eerdmans, Grand Rapids, MI, 1968.

To obtain inductive Bible studies based on this material,
which can be used for your personal study or for small group studies,
simply e-mail your request to: Larry@covenantlifepc.com
At your request, we'll also be glad to email you
a multi-page explanation of the paintings.

To order additional copies of

Have your credit card ready and call

Toll free: (877) 421-READ (7323)

or send $16.99* each plus $3.95 S&H**
(Please ask for your 30% discount when ordering 5 copies or more)

to
WinePress Publishing
PO Box 428
Enumclaw, WA 98022

*Washington residents please add 8.4% tax.
**Add $1.00 S&H for each additional book ordered.